What the
BIBLE
Says
about
MARRIAGE

What the
BIBLE
Says
about
MARRIAGE

BARBOUR
PUBLISHING

Published by Barbour Publishing, Inc., P.O. Box 719, Uhrichsville, Ohio 44683, www.barbourbooks.com

Our mission is to publish and distribute inspirational products offering exceptional value and biblical encouragement to the masses.

ecpa Member of the
Evangelical Christian
Publishers Association

Printed in the United States of America

CONTENTS

INTRODUCTION

"AND THEY LIVED HAPPILY EVER AFTER."

That romantic line concludes many make-believe stories in which a man and woman enjoy endless, warm emotions and a trouble-free life. The problem is that real-life marriages don't unfold between the covers of a fairy-tale book. While many couples hold on to this unrealistic ideal, most marriages in the world cannot be classified as "happy."

Contrary to Hollywood's presentations, successful marriages are maintained by choices—not by feelings. The decision to remain faithful is deliberate. The choice to put your spouse's interests ahead of your own is often a conscious one.

Whether you're a newlywed or have been married for decades, you can learn much from the Bible about marriage and successful human relationships. Read through the following collection of Bible verses and begin finding God's wisdom for improving your marriage.

CHAPTER 1

DEFINING MARRIAGE

"One flesh." That phrase grabbed me during
a recent wedding I attended. Imagine what it
would be like to actually attain "oneness" with
someone physically, emotionally, and spiritually.
While my husband and I share some values and
some general dreams, there are a number of
areas where I simply live my life and he lives his.
I suppose that's natural to some extent. But that
wedding has got me thinking: should our lives
overlap more? Are there additional core
values we should be sharing?

■ Ashley, age 48, Montana ■

ACHIEVING ONENESS

■ And this is why a man leaves father and
mother and cherishes his wife. No longer
two, they become "one flesh." This is a huge
mystery, and I don't pretend to understand
it all.

EPHESIANS 5:31–32 MSG

■ So God created man in his own image,
in the image of God he created him;
male and female he created them.

God blessed them and said to them,
"Be fruitful and increase in number;
fill the earth and subdue it. Rule over the
fish of the sea and the birds of the air and
over every living creature that moves on
the ground."

GENESIS 1:27–28 NIV

■ Life is short, and you love your wife, so enjoy being with her. This is what you are supposed to do as you struggle through life on this earth.

ECCLESIASTES 9:9 CEV

■ I want them to be encouraged and knit together by strong ties of love. I want them to have complete confidence that they understand God's mysterious plan, which is Christ himself.

COLOSSIANS 2:2 NLT

■ "For where two or three are gathered in my name, I am there among them."

MATTHEW 18:20 NRSV

■ You do well when you complete the Royal
Rule of the Scriptures: "Love others as you
love yourself."

JAMES 2:8 MSG

■ No one has ever seen God; if we love one
another, God lives in us, and his love is
perfected in us.

1 JOHN 4:12 NRSV

■ How wonderful and pleasant it is
when brothers live together in harmony!

PSALM 133:1 NLT

■ You were all called to travel on the same road and in the same direction, so stay together, both outwardly and inwardly. You have one Master, one faith, one baptism, one God and Father of all, who rules over all, works through all, and is present in all. Everything you are and think and do is permeated with Oneness.

EPHESIANS 4:4–6 MSG

SUBMITTING TO EACH OTHER

■ And further, submit to one another out of reverence for Christ. For wives, this means submit to your husbands as to the Lord. For a husband is the head of his wife as Christ is the head of the church. He is the Savior of his body, the church. As the church submits to Christ, so you wives should submit to your husbands in everything. For husbands, this means love your wives, just as Christ loved the church. He gave up his life for her.

EPHESIANS 5:21–25 NLT

■ Let us then pursue what makes for peace and for mutual upbuilding.

ROMANS 14:19 NRSV

■ Is there any encouragement from belonging to Christ? Any comfort from his love? Any fellowship together in the Spirit? Are your hearts tender and compassionate? Then make me truly happy by agreeing wholeheartedly with each other, loving one another, and working together with one mind and purpose. Don't be selfish; don't try to impress others. Be humble, thinking of others as better than yourselves. Don't look out only for your own interests, but take an interest in others, too. You must have the same attitude that Christ Jesus had.

PHILIPPIANS 2:1–5 NLT

■ In the same way, husbands ought to love their wives as they love their own bodies. For a man who loves his wife actually shows love for himself. No one hates his own body but feeds and cares for it, just as Christ cares for the church. And we are members of his body. . . So again I say, each man must love his wife as he loves himself, and the wife must respect her husband.

EPHESIANS 5:28–30, 33 NLT

■ "Here is a simple rule of thumb for behavior: Ask yourself what you want people to do for you; then grab the initiative and do it for them!"

LUKE 6:31 MSG

■ But Jesus called the disciples together and said:
You know that foreign rulers like to order their people around. And their great leaders have full power over everyone they rule. But don't act like them. If you want to be great, you must be the servant of all the others. And if you want to be first, you must be the slave of the rest. The Son of Man did not come to be a slave master, but a slave who will give his life to rescue many people.

MATTHEW 20:25–28 CEV

■ However, each one of you also must love his wife as he loves himself, and the wife must respect her husband.

EPHESIANS 5:33 NIV

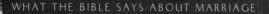

■ Wives, understand and support your husbands by submitting to them in ways that honor the Master.

COLOSSIANS 3:18 MSG

■ As God's chosen ones, holy and beloved, clothe yourselves with compassion, kindness, humility, meekness, and patience.

COLOSSIANS 3:12 NRSV

SHARING A VISION

■ It's better to have a partner than go it alone.
Share the work, share the wealth.
And if one falls down, the other helps,
but if there's no one to help, tough!

ECCLESIASTES 4:9–10 MSG

■ Can two walk together, unless they are
agreed?

AMOS 3:3 NKJV

■ By yourself you're unprotected.
With a friend you can face the worst.
Can you round up a third?
A three-stranded rope isn't easily snapped.

ECCLESIASTES 4:12 MSG

■ As iron sharpens iron, so a friend sharpens a friend.

PROVERBS 27:17 NLT

■ But more than anything else, put God's work first and do what he wants. Then the other things will be yours as well.

Don't worry about tomorrow. It will take care of itself. You have enough to worry about today.

MATTHEW 6:33–34 CEV

■ Commit your works to the LORD
And your plans will be established.

PROVERBS 16:3 NASB

■ "For I know the plans I have for you," says
the Lord. "They are plans for good and not
for disaster, to give you a future and a hope.
In those days when you pray, I will listen.
If you look for me wholeheartedly, you will
find me."

JEREMIAH 29:11–13 NLT

■ That is what the Scriptures mean when
they say,
"No eye has seen, no ear has heard,
and no mind has imagined what God
has prepared for those who love him."

1 CORINTHIANS 2:9 NLT

ONE MOMENT
AT A TIME

BECOMING ONE

■ 1. Face the size of the task. Succeeding at marriage is difficult and should not be taken lightly. Commit yourself to the active and ongoing task of making your relationship a success. If you let your marriage mature by chance, it is unlikely to succeed.

■ 2. Evaluate against the right standard. If you compare yourself with friends, you probably have a better marriage than some of them. Compare yourself, however, with the standard God gave. In what ways does your marriage model Christ's relationship with the church? In what ways do you need to improve?

3. Pursue oneness. Because both you and your spouse are human, it's unlikely that you'll achieve perfect unity. Still, marriages where both partners are working toward similar goals tend to be healthier than those where each spouse is concerned only for one's own plans and dreams. Find an area or two where you and your spouse do well. Continue to improve that strength. Isolate an area where you could stand to improve. Go to dinner or take a weekend away to discuss ways you might grow together.

CHAPTER 2

TRUE LOVE

On any given day, the amount of affection
I feel for my husband can swing as wildly as
my blood sugar levels. A fond memory can
make my stomach jump like a school girl
but that can quickly fade into annoyance
as I pick up his dirty socks again.
Sometimes the swings concern me.
Am I normal?

■ Joanna, age 32, Utah ■

DEFINING LOVE

■ Dear children, let's not merely say that we love each other; let us show the truth by our actions.

1 JOHN 3:18 NLT

■ Such love has no fear, because perfect love expels all fear. If we are afraid, it is for fear of punishment, and this shows that we have not fully experienced his perfect love.

1 JOHN 4:18 NLT

■ For husbands, this means love your wives, just as Christ loved the church. He gave up his life for her.

EPHESIANS 5:25 NLT

If I speak in the tongues of men and of angels, but have not love, I am only a resounding gong or a clanging cymbal. If I have the gift of prophecy and can fathom all mysteries and all knowledge, and if I have a faith that can move mountains, but have not love, I am nothing. If I give all I possess to the poor and surrender my body to the flames, but have not love, I gain nothing.

Love is patient, love is kind. It does not envy, it does not boast, it is not proud. It is not rude, it is not self-seeking, it is not easily angered, it keeps no record of wrongs. Love does not delight in evil but rejoices with the truth. It always protects, always trusts, always hopes, always perseveres.

Love never fails.

1 CORINTHIANS 13:1–8 NIV

■ Above all, clothe yourselves with love, which binds us all together in perfect harmony. And let the peace that comes from Christ rule in your hearts. For as members of one body you are called to live in peace. And always be thankful.

COLOSSIANS 3:14–15 NLT

■ "'Love others as much as you love yourself.' No other commandment is more important than these."

MARK 12:31 CEV

■ There is no greater love than to lay down one's life for one's friends.

JOHN 15:13 NLT

BEING STEADFAST

■ Now it is required that those who have been given a trust must prove faithful.

1 CORINTHIANS 4:2 NIV

■ Many will say they are loyal friends, but who can find one who is truly reliable?

PROVERBS 20:6 NLT

■ Love the LORD, all his saints!
   The LORD preserves the faithful,
      but the proud he pays back in full.

PSALM 31:23 NIV

■ God blesses his loyal people.

PROVERBS 28:20 CEV

■ "Whoever can be trusted with very little
   can also be trusted with much, and whoever
   is dishonest with very little will also be
   dishonest with much."

LUKE 16:10 NIV

■ Do you know the saying, "Drink from your
      own rain barrel, draw water from your
      own spring-fed well"?
   It's true. Otherwise, you may one day come
      home and find your barrel empty and
      your well polluted.

PROVERBS 5:15–16 MSG

■ "But at the beginning of creation God 'made them male and female.' 'For this reason a man will leave his father and mother and be united to his wife, and the two will become one flesh.' So they are no longer two, but one. Therefore what God has joined together, let man not separate."

MARK 10:6–9 NIV

■ Do not let loyalty and faithfulness forsake you;
  bind them around your neck,
  write them on the tablet of your heart.
So you will find favor and good repute
  in the sight of God and of people.

PROVERBS 3:3–4 NRSV

■ For the LORD loves justice;
  he will not forsake his saints.
They are preserved forever,
  but the children of the wicked shall
  be cut off.

PSALM 37:28 ESV

■ "To the faithful you show yourself faithful;
to those with integrity you show integrity."

2 SAMUEL 22:26 NLT

■ For example, by law a married woman is
bound to her husband as long as he is alive,
but if her husband dies, she is released from
the law of marriage.

ROMANS 7:2 NIV

SHOWING AFFECTION

■ Don't just pretend to love others. Really love them. Hate what is wrong. Hold tightly to what is good. Love each other with genuine affection, and take delight in honoring each other.

ROMANS 12:9–10 NLT

■ The light of the eyes rejoices the heart,
    And good news refreshes the body.

PROVERBS 15:30 NRSV

■ And since I, your Lord and Teacher, have washed your feet, you ought to wash each other's feet. I have given you an example to follow. Do as I have done to you.

JOHN 13:14–15 NLT

■ So it is right that I should feel as I do about all of you, for you have a special place in my heart. You share with me the special favor of God, both in my imprisonment and in defending and confirming the truth of the Good News.

PHILIPPIANS 1:7 NLT

■ A glad heart makes a cheerful countenance, but by sorrow of heart the spirit is broken.

PROVERBS 15:13 NRSV

■ For I have derived much joy and comfort from your love, my brother, because the hearts of the saints have been refreshed through you.

PHILEMON 1:7 ESV

■ We loved you so much that we were delighted to share with you not only the gospel of God but our lives as well, because you had become so dear to us.

1 THESSALONIANS 2:8 NIV

ONE MOMENT
AT A TIME

LEARNING
TO LOVE

1. Redefine love. Love is not just a feeling but a purposeful decision to be kind and sacrificial to the other person. Love is something you can choose to show no matter what you are feeling toward your spouse.

2. Allow affection to follow. Once you've been married for a while, the degree of affection you feel toward your spouse can vary. Whether you feel giddy or lethargic, make it your goal to live so that your spouse doesn't sense a difference because of your actions. You'll find that as you act lovingly, the warm emotions may follow.

3. Be committed. There may be moments that you fantasize about being married to someone else or you may look back at your courtship and wonder if you married the right person. While doubts are natural, don't let them get in the way of the commitment you've made. Unless you are in an abusive situation, recommit to stay in your marriage. Don't linger on the dangerous daydreams. Instead, focus on your spouse and on your life together.

WHAT THE BIBLE SAYS ABOUT MARRIAGE

CHAPTER 3

YOU AND YOUR SPOUSE

I got married late. Some of my friends said I had a fear of commitment. Others said I loved my job too much. The truth is, I got married late because I was holding out for Mr. Perfect. It wasn't until I was approaching forty that I finally realized that Mr. Perfect didn't exist. While I love my new husband and our life together, I often counsel perfectionistic, young women to be less picky. Sometimes it's enough if the man is headed in the right direction, loves Jesus, and puts you first. I've come to realize that they don't get much more perfect than that.

■ Krista, age 40, California ■

DEFINING THE IDEAL MAN

- Better a poor man whose walk is blameless
  than a rich man whose ways are perverse.

  PROVERBS 28:6 NIV

- The righteous man leads a blameless life;
  blessed are his children after him.

  PROVERBS 20:7 NIV

- The man of integrity walks securely,
  but he who takes crooked paths will be
  found out.

  PROVERBS 10:9 NIV

■ But there are preconditions: A leader must be well-thought-of, committed to his wife, cool and collected, accessible, and hospitable. He must know what he's talking about, not be overfond of wine, not pushy but gentle, not thin-skinned, not money-hungry. He must handle his own affairs well, attentive to his own children and having their respect. For if someone is unable to handle his own affairs, how can he take care of God's church? He must not be a new believer, lest the position go to his head and the Devil trip him up. Outsiders must think well of him, or else the Devil will figure out a way to lure him into his trap.

1 TIMOTHY 3:2–7 MSG

■ Blessed is the man who finds wisdom,
the man who gains understanding,
for she is more profitable than silver
and yields better returns than gold.

PROVERBS 3:13–14 NIV

■ A man's pride brings him low,
but a man of lowly spirit gains honor.

PROVERBS 29:23 NIV

DEFINING THE IDEAL WOMAN

- Charm is deceptive, and beauty does not last; but a woman who fears the LORD will be greatly praised.

    PROVERBS 31:30 NLT

- Similarly, teach the older women to live in a way that honors God. They must not slander others or be heavy drinkers. Instead, they should teach others what is good. These older women must train the younger women to love their husbands and their children, to live wisely and be pure, to work in their homes, to do good, and to be submissive to their husbands. Then they will not bring shame on the word of God.

    TITUS 2:3–5 NLT

■ Who can find a virtuous and capable wife?
She is more precious than rubies. Her
husband can trust her, and she will greatly
enrich his life. She brings him good, not
harm, all the days of her life. She finds wool
and flax and busily spins it. She is like a
merchant's ship, bringing her food from
afar. She gets up before dawn to prepare
breakfast for her household and plan the
day's work for her servant girls. She goes
to inspect a field and buys it; with her earn-
ings she plants a vineyard. She is energetic
and strong, a hard worker. She makes sure
her dealings are profitable; her lamp burns
late into the night. Her hands are busy
spinning thread, her fingers twisting fiber.
She extends a helping hand to the poor
and opens her arms to the needy. She has
no fear of winter for her household, for
everyone has warm clothes. She makes her
own bedspreads. She dresses in fine linen
and purple gowns. . . .

She is clothed with strength and dignity, and she laughs without fear of the future. When she speaks, her words are wise, and she gives instructions with kindness. She carefully watches everything in her household and suffers nothing from laziness.

PROVERBS 31:10–22, 25–27 NLT

A kindhearted woman gains respect, but ruthless men gain only wealth.

PROVERBS 11:16 NIV

A helpful wife is a jewel for her husband, but a shameless wife will make his bones rot.

PROVERBS 12:4 CEV

■ A woman's family is held together by her wisdom, but it can be destroyed by her foolishness.

PROVERBS 14:1 CEV

ASPIRING TO BE A GODLY MATE

■ Rather train yourself for godliness.

1 TIMOTHY 4:7 ESV

■ Like newborn babies, crave pure spiritual milk, so that by it you may grow up in your salvation.

1 PETER 2:2 NIV

■ God blesses those people who want to obey him more than to eat or drink. They will be given what they want!

MATTHEW 5:6 CEV

■ Dear friends, I urge you, as aliens and strangers in the world, to abstain from sinful desires, which war against your soul.

1 PETER 2:11 NIV

■ So I say, let the Holy Spirit guide your lives. Then you won't be doing what your sinful nature craves.

GALATIANS 5:16 NLT

■ But the Holy Spirit produces this kind of fruit in our lives: love, joy, peace, patience, kindness, goodness, faithfulness, gentleness, and self-control. There is no law against these things!

GALATIANS 5:22–23 NLT

■ And we are instructed to turn from godless living and sinful pleasures. We should live in this evil world with wisdom, righteousness, and devotion to God.

TITUS 2:12 NLT

■ Avoid every kind of evil.

1 THESSALONIANS 5:22 NIV

■ Dear friends, God is good. So I beg you to offer your bodies to him as a living sacrifice, pure and pleasing. That's the most sensible way to serve God. Don't be like the people of this world, but let God change the way you think. Then you will know how to do everything that is good and pleasing to him.

ROMANS 12:1–2 CEV

■ In view of all this, make every effort to respond to God's promises. Supplement your faith with a generous provision of moral excellence, and moral excellence with knowledge, and knowledge with self-control, and self-control with patient endurance, and patient endurance with godliness, and godliness with brotherly affection, and brotherly affection with love for everyone. The more you grow like this, the more productive and useful you will be in your knowledge of our Lord Jesus Christ.

2 PETER 1:5–8 NLT

■ In this way, you may know the truth and take an accurate report to those who sent you.

PROVERBS 22:21 NLT

■ Let us cleanse ourselves from all filthiness of the flesh and spirit, perfecting holiness in the fear of God.

2 CORINTHIANS 7:1 NKJV

■ Since everything around us is going to be destroyed like this, what holy and godly lives you should live, looking forward to the day of God and hurrying it along. On that day, he will set the heavens on fire, and the elements will melt away in the flames. But we are looking forward to the new heavens and new earth he has promised, a world filled with God's righteousness. And so, dear friends, while you are waiting for these things to happen, make every effort to be found living peaceful lives that are pure and blame-less in his sight.

2 PETER 3:11–14 NLT

■ Anyone who claims to be intimate with
God ought to live the same kind of life
Jesus lived.

1 JOHN 2:6 MSG

■ God is not unjust; he will not forget your
work and the love you have shown him as
you have helped his people and continue
to help them. We want each of you to show
this same diligence to the very end, in order
to make your hope sure. We do not want
you to become lazy, but to imitate those
who through faith and patience inherit what
has been promised.

HEBREWS 6:10–12 NIV

■ Now may the God of peace make you holy in every way, and may your whole spirit and soul and body be kept blameless until our Lord Jesus Christ comes again.

1 THESSALONIANS 5:23 NLT

WHAT THE BIBLE SAYS ABOUT MARRIAGE

LOOKING BEYOND YOUR SPOUSE'S FAULTS

■ Always be humble and gentle. Patiently put up with each other and love each other. Try your best to let God's Spirit keep your hearts united. Do this by living at peace.

EPHESIANS 4:2–3 CEV

■ "Pay attention to yourselves! If your brother sins, rebuke him, and if he repents, forgive him, and if he sins against you seven times in the day, and turns to you seven times, saying, 'I repent,' you must forgive him."

LUKE 17:3–4 ESV

■ If you forgive others for the wrongs they do to you, your Father in heaven will forgive you.

MATTHEW 6:14 CEV

■ He who covers a transgression seeks love,
But he who repeats a matter separates
friends.

PROVERBS 17:9 NKJV

■ "If your brother sins against you, go and tell
him his fault, between you and him alone.
If he listens to you, you have gained your
brother."

MATTHEW 18:15 ESV

■ Hatred stirs up strife,
but love covers all offenses.

PROVERBS 10:12 NRSV

■ Be kind and compassionate to one another,
forgiving each other, just as in Christ God
forgave you.

EPHESIANS 4:32 NIV

57

■ So now I am giving you a new commandment: Love each other. Just as I have loved
you, you should love each other.

JOHN 13:34 NLT

■ "Be merciful, just as your Father is merciful."

LUKE 6:36 NIV

■ Your kindness will reward you, but your
cruelty will destroy you.

PROVERBS 11:17 NLT

■ So if you are about to place your gift on the
altar and remember that someone is angry
with you, leave your gift there in front of
the altar. Make peace with that person, then
come back and offer your gift to God.

MATTHEW 5:23–24 CEV

SUPPORTING EACH OTHER

■ Share each other's burdens, and in this way obey the law of Christ.

GALATIANS 6:2 NLT

■ If one part of our body hurts, we hurt all over. If one part of our body is honored, the whole body will be happy.

1 CORINTHIANS 12:26 CEV

■ Be devoted to one another in brotherly love. Honor one another above yourselves.

ROMANS 12:10 NIV

■ Let's see how inventive we can be in encouraging love and helping out.

HEBREWS 10:24 MSG

■ It's better to have a partner than go it alone.
Share the work, share the wealth.
And if one falls down, the other helps,
But if there's no one to help, tough!
Two in a bed warm each other.
Alone, you shiver all night.
By yourself you're unprotected.
With a friend you can face the worst.
Can you round up a third?
A three-stranded rope isn't easily snapped.

ECCLESIASTES 4:9–12 MSG

■ Jesus replied: "'Love the Lord your God with all your heart and with all your soul and with all your mind.' This is the first and greatest commandment. And the second is like it: 'Love your neighbor as yourself.' All the Law and the Prophets hang on these two commandments."

MATTHEW 22:37–40 NIV

RESPECTING YOUR SPOUSE

■ These older women must train the younger
women to love their husbands and their
children, to live wisely and be pure, to
work in their homes, to do good, and to
be submissive to their husbands. Then
they will not bring shame on the word
of God.

TITUS 2:4–5 NLT

■ Husbands, in the same way be considerate
as you live with your wives, and treat them
with respect as the weaker partner and as
heirs with you of the gracious gift of life, so
that nothing will hinder your prayers.

1 PETER 3:7 NIV

LIVING WITH AN UNBELIEVING SPOUSE

■ Instead, you must worship Christ as Lord of your life. And if someone asks about your Christian hope, always be ready to explain it. But do this in a gentle and respectful way. Keep your conscience clear. Then if people speak against you, they will be ashamed when they see what a good life you live because you belong to Christ.

1 PETER 3:15–16 NLT

■ Wives, in the same way be submissive to your husbands so that, if any of them do not believe the word, they may be won over without words by the behavior of their wives, when they see the purity and reverence of your lives.

1 PETER 3:1–2 NIV

63

■ "Let me tell you why you are here. You're here to be salt-seasoning that brings out the God-flavors of this earth. If you lose your saltiness, how will people taste godliness? You've lost your usefulness and will end up in the garbage. Here's another way to put it: You're here to be light, bringing out the God-colors in the world. God is not a secret to be kept. We're going public with this, as public as a city on a hill."

MATTHEW 5:13–14 MSG

■ Let your light so shine before men, that they may see your good works and glorify your Father in heaven.

MATTHEW 5:16 NKJV

■ Now, I will speak to the rest of you, though I do not have a direct command from the Lord. If a Christian man has a wife who is not a believer and she is willing to continue living with him, he must not leave her. And if a Christian woman has a husband who is not a believer and he is willing to continue living with her, she must not leave him. For the Christian wife brings holiness to her marriage, and the Christian husband brings holiness to his marriage. Otherwise, your children would not be holy, but now they are holy. (But if the husband or wife who isn't a believer insists on leaving, let them go. In such cases the Christian husband or wife is no longer bound to the other, for God has called you to live in peace.) Don't you wives realize that your husbands might be saved because of you? And don't you husbands realize that your wives might be saved because of you?

1 CORINTHIANS 7:12–16 NLT

ONE MOMENT
AT A TIME

LIVING
TOGETHER

1. Count your blessings first. Rather than become obsessed with your spouse's weaknesses, devote some time in your daily prayer to thank God for some specific strengths that you value in your spouse.

2. Remember that neither of you is perfect. Sure, it's easy to point out the faults of your partner but you have your own weaknesses, too. Focus on fixing yourself before you set out to improve your spouse.

3. Evaluate yourself humbly. Don't take an "I'll fix this about me, if you fix that about you" attitude. Ask your spouse to help you identify and work on a specific weakness in your own life.

4. Demonstrate Christ's love every day. Whether or not your spouse is a Christian, work hard at showing him or her the love Christ has shown you.

CHAPTER 4

DIVORCE AND REMARRIAGE

I have no doubt that my first marriage was a mistake. She was the wrong girl and I was certainly the wrong guy. While I was a Christian at the time, I was pretty immature and self-absorbed. I was quick to blame my wife for every conflict we faced. The divorce came quickly and she remarried within a few months. As for me, I've thought about getting remarried but my guilt lingers. Has God forgiven me for the role I played in that failure? Would God be okay with my giving marriage another shot?

■ Jeremy, age 26, New York ■

AVOIDING DIVORCE

■ But for those who are married, I have a command that comes not from me, but from the Lord. A wife must not leave her husband. But if she does leave him, let her remain single or else be reconciled to him. And the husband must not leave his wife.

1 CORINTHIANS 7:10–11 NLT

■ "You have heard the law that says, 'A man can divorce his wife by merely giving her a written notice of divorce.' But I say that a man who divorces his wife, unless she has been unfaithful, causes her to commit adultery. And anyone who marries a divorced woman also commits adultery."

MATTHEW 5:31–32 NLT

■ "Haven't you read the Scriptures?" Jesus replied. "They record that from the beginning 'God made them male and female.' And he said, 'This explains why a man leaves his father and mother and is joined to his wife, and the two are united into one.' Since they are no longer two but one, let no one split apart what God has joined together."

MATTHEW 19:4–6 NLT

■ "I hate divorce," says the LORD God of Israel.

MALACHI 2:16 NIV

■ Above all, love each other deeply, because love covers over a multitude of sins.

1 PETER 4:8 NIV

■ Jesus replied, "Moses permitted divorce only as a concession to your hard hearts, but it was not what God had originally intended. And I tell you this, whoever divorces his wife and marries someone else commits adultery— unless his wife has been unfaithful."

Jesus' disciples then said to him, "If this is the case, it is better not to marry!"

"Not everyone can accept this statement," Jesus said. "Only those whom God helps. Some are born as eunuchs, some have been made eunuchs by others, and some choose not to marry for the sake of the Kingdom of Heaven. Let anyone accept this who can."

MATTHEW 19:8–12 NLT

■ Finishing is better than starting. Patience is better than pride.

Control your temper, for anger labels you a fool.

ECCLESIASTES 7:8–9 NLT

BECOMING REMARRIED

■ Here is my advice for people who have never
been married and for widows. You should
stay single, just as I am. But if you don't have
enough self-control, then go ahead and get
married. After all, it is better to marry than
to burn with desire.

1 CORINTHIANS 7:8–9 CEV

■ A righteous man is cautious in friendship,
but the way of the wicked leads them astray.

PROVERBS 12:26 NIV

■ Those who trust their own insight are foolish,
but anyone who walks in wisdom is safe.

PROVERBS 28:26 NLT

■ Stay away from people who are not follow-
ers of the Lord! Can someone who is good
get along with someone who is evil? Are light
and darkness the same? Is Christ a friend of
Satan? Can people who follow the Lord have
anything in common with those who don't?

2 CORINTHIANS 6:14–15 CEV

■ He who finds a wife finds a good thing,
and obtains favor from the Lord.

PROVERBS 18:22 NRSV

■ You may inherit all you own from your
parents, but a sensible wife is a gift from
the LORD.

PROVERBS 19:14 CEV

■ Trust in the LORD and do good;

> dwell in the land and enjoy safe pasture.

Delight yourself in the LORD and he will

> give you the desires of your heart.

Commit your way to the LORD;

> trust in him and he will do this.

PSALM 37:3–5 NIV

ONE MOMENT
AT A TIME

CONSIDERING
REMARRIAGE

■ 1. Divorce is not the unforgivable sin. If you
have been divorced, there were probably
plenty of sinful actions, thoughts, and attitudes
on both sides of the table. It is important to
remember that God forgives His children
more than they deserve. God's forgiveness
is complete and final.

■ 2. Consider a time to move on. Reconciliation with your ex can be a God-honoring
goal. If that goal is in your heart and your
ex-spouse is open to it, then keep the
matter in prayer and take steps to see if it
is reasonable. If your spouse has moved on,

it is important that you don't hold on to an unrealistic dream so that it cripples your life. If your previous marriage is over, then you may need to accept the finality of that fact and move on with your life.

3. Don't point fingers. Most marriages end with each party thinking that the ex-spouse was primarily to blame for the collapse of the relationship. Sit with a pastor or a close friend and focus instead on yourself. What can your divorce experience teach you? How can you become a better friend (or perhaps even a better spouse) in the future?

CHAPTER 5

COMMUNICATION

How can my wife not know that her
spending drives me crazy? Sure, I understand
that day trips and vacations build memories
for the kids, but does it really require so much?
To be honest, though, I can't even discuss it
with her without my blood pressure going
through the roof. We've got to talk about
it soon or we'll go broke.

■ Miguel, age 53, Tennessee ■

COMMUNICATING WELL

■ Don't use foul or abusive language.
Let everything you say be good and helpful,
so that your words will be an encouragement
to those who hear them.

EPHESIANS 4:29 NLT

■ Fools show their anger at once,
but the prudent ignore an insult.

PROVERBS 12:16 NRSV

■ Therefore each of you must put off falsehood
and speak truthfully to his neighbor, for we
are all members of one body.

EPHESIANS 4:25 NIV

■ Obscene stories, foolish talk, and coarse
jokes—these are not for you. Instead,
let there be thankfulness to God.

EPHESIANS 5:4 NLT

■ Timely advice is lovely, like golden apples
in a silver basket.
To one who listens, valid criticism is like a
gold earring or other gold jewelry.

PROVERBS 25:11–12 NLT

■ May the words of my mouth and the
meditation of my heart be pleasing in your
sight, O LORD, my Rock and my Redeemer.

PSALM 19:14 NIV

LISTENING WELL

■ A truly wise person uses few words; a person
with understanding is even-tempered.

PROVERBS 17:27 NLT

■ Do you see someone who is hasty in speech?
There is more hope for a fool than for
anyone like that.

PROVERBS 29:20 NRSV

■ Answering before listening is both stupid
and rude.

PROVERBS 18:13 MSG

■ A fool gives full vent to anger,
but the wise quietly holds it back.

PROVERBS 29:11 NRSV

■ "Why do you look at the speck of sawdust in your brother's eye and pay no attention to the plank in your own eye?"

MATTHEW 7:3 NIV

■ Know this, my beloved brothers: let every person be quick to hear, slow to speak, slow to anger.

JAMES 1:19 ESV

■ When words are many, sin is not absent, but he who holds his tongue is wise.

PROVERBS 10:19 NIV

■ Watch your tongue and keep your mouth shut, and you will stay out of trouble.

PROVERBS 21:23 NLT

HANDLING CONFLICT

■ Husbands, love your wives and never treat them harshly.

COLOSSIANS 3:19 NLT

■ Whoever is slow to anger has great understanding, but he who has a hasty temper exalts folly.

PROVERBS 14:29 ESV

■ If you churn milk
you get butter;
if you pound on your nose,
you get blood—
and if you stay angry,
you get in trouble.

PROVERBS 30:33 CEV

■ Don't hit back; discover beauty in everyone.

ROMANS 12:17 MSG

■ Do not gloat when your enemy falls;
when he stumbles, do not let your heart
rejoice, or the LORD will see and disapprove.

PROVERBS 24:17–18 NIV

■ Rash words are like sword thrusts,
but the tongue of the wise brings healing.

PROVERBS 12:18 NRSV

■ Therefore encourage one another and build
each other up, just as in fact you are doing.

1 THESSALONIANS 5:11 NIV

AVOIDING SQUABBLES

■ Work at living in peace with everyone, and work at living a holy life, for those who are not holy will not see the Lord.

HEBREWS 12:14 NLT

■ Greed causes fighting; trusting the LORD leads to prosperity.

PROVERBS 28:25 NLT

■ Sensible people control their temper; they earn respect by overlooking wrongs.

PROVERBS 19:11 NLT

■ A gentle answer turns away wrath,
but a harsh word stirs up anger.

PROVERBS 15:1 NIV

■ Starting a quarrel is like breaching a dam;
    so drop the matter before a dispute
    breaks out.

PROVERBS 17:14 NIV

■ "Do not judge others, and you will not be
judged. For you will be treated as you treat
others. The standard you use in judging is the
standard by which you will be judged. And
why worry about a speck in your friend's eye
when you have a log in your own? How can
you think of saying to your friend, 'Let me
help you get rid of that speck in your eye,'
when you can't see past the log in your own
eye? Hypocrite! First get rid of the log in your
own eye; then you will see well enough to
deal with the speck in your friend's eye."

MATTHEW 7:1–5 NLT

■ Blessed are the peacemakers, for they will be called sons of God.

MATTHEW 5:9 NIV

■ The hotheaded do things they'll later regret; the coldhearted get the cold shoulder.

PROVERBS 14:17 MSG

■ A quarrelsome person in a dispute is like kerosene thrown on a fire.

PROVERBS 26:21 MSG

■ Anyone who loves to quarrel loves sin; anyone who trusts in high walls invites disaster.

PROVERBS 17:19 NLT

■ Peacemakers who sow in peace raise a
harvest of righteousness.

JAMES 3:18 NIV

■ Kind words are like honey—sweet to the
soul and healthy for the body.

PROVERBS 16:24 NLT

■ Better a dry crust eaten in peace than a
house filled with feasting—and conflict.

PROVERBS 17:1 NLT

■ What causes fights and quarrels among you?
Don't they come from your desires that
battle within you?

JAMES 4:1 NIV

ONE MOMENT
AT A TIME

DEALING WITH CONFLICT

■ 1. Listen. It takes humility and restraint to listen without justifying yourself or defending your actions. Become a great listener. Learn to lose an argument rather than winning at all costs.

■ 2. Don't expect mindreading. Many conflicts occur because the expectations aren't clear. Does your spouse know the things that drive you crazy? Or do you get upset when he or she hasn't lived up to expectations you've never communicated?

3. Get off-site. Do you have a topic that needs to be discussed? Perhaps something regarding money? Or something else regarding the kids? Try going off-site rather than talking at home. Discussing your topic over coffee at a neutral location can help discharge the situation.

CHAPTER 6

ANGER AND ABUSE

When we were dating, I thought it was sweet
that he got jealous. I liked that he paid such close
attention to what I wear and who I spend time
with. I couldn't believe that such an amazing,
perfect guy would want to be with me. But now
that we've been married awhile, I'm not so sure.
He gets really upset when I talk too much to
anyone else. He says nasty things about certain
clothes I wear. It seems like I can't do anything
right. Everything I do makes him angry.
Maybe it is my fault. Maybe I have no reason
to feel afraid—but I do.

■ Madeline, age 36, Arkansas ■

DEALING WITH ANGER

■ A hot-tempered person starts fights;
a cool-tempered person stops them.

PROVERBS 15:18 NLT

■ Be patient and trust the LORD. Don't let it
bother you when all goes well for those who
do sinful things.

Don't be angry or furious. Anger can lead
to sin.

PSALM 37:7–8 CEV

■ Don't get so angry that you sin. Don't go to
bed angry.

EPHESIANS 4:26 CEV

■ Only fools get angry quickly and hold a
grudge.

ECCLESIASTES 7:9 CEV

■ "I'm telling you that anyone who is so much
as angry with a brother or sister is guilty of
murder. Carelessly call a brother 'idiot!' and
you just might find yourself hauled into court.
Thoughtlessly yell 'stupid!' at a sister and you
are on the brink of hellfire. The simple moral
fact is that words kill."

MATTHEW 5:22 MSG

■ But now you must stop doing such things.
You must quit being angry, hateful, and evil.
You must no longer say insulting or cruel
things about others.

COLOSSIANS 3:8 CEV

■ Don't befriend angry people or associate with hot-tempered people, or you will learn to be like them and endanger your soul.

PROVERBS 22:24–25 NLT

■ Beloved, never avenge yourselves, but leave it to the wrath of God, for it is written, "Vengeance is mine, I will repay, says the Lord." To the contrary, "if your enemy is hungry, feed him; if he is thirsty, give him something to drink; for by so doing you will heap burning coals on his head." Do not be overcome by evil, but overcome evil with good.

ROMANS 12:19–21 ESV

■ If you see your enemy hungry, go buy him lunch; if he's thirsty, bring him a drink.

Your generosity will surprise him with goodness, and GOD will look after you.

PROVERBS 25:21–22 MSG

■ "Blessed are those who are persecuted because of righteousness, for theirs is the kingdom of heaven.

Blessed are you when people insult you, persecute you and falsely say all kinds of evil against you because of me. Rejoice and be glad, because great is your reward in heaven, for in the same way they persecuted the prophets who were before you."

MATTHEW 5:10–12 NIV

■ Let all bitterness and wrath and anger and clamor and slander be put away from you, along with all malice.

EPHESIANS 4:31 ESV

■ Better to be patient than powerful; better to have self-control than to conquer a city.

PROVERBS 16:32 NLT

■ Fools have short fuses and explode all too quickly; the prudent quietly shrug off insults.

PROVERBS 12:16 MSG

RESISTING BITTERNESS

■ See to it that no one misses the grace of God and that no bitter root grows up to cause trouble and defile many.

HEBREWS 12:15 NIV

■ Above all else, guard your heart,
　　for it is the wellspring of life.

PROVERBS 4:23 NIV

■ Anyone who claims to be in the light but hates his brother is still in the darkness. Whoever loves his brother lives in the light, and there is nothing in him to make him stumble. But whoever hates his brother is in the darkness and walks around in the darkness; he does not know where he is going, because the darkness has blinded him.

1 JOHN 2:9–11 NIV

WHAT THE BIBLE SAYS ABOUT MARRIAGE

■ Don't grumble against each other, brothers,
or you will be judged. The Judge is standing
at the door!

JAMES 5:9 NIV

■ People may cover their hatred with pleasant
words, but they're deceiving you.

They pretend to be kind, but don't
believe them. Their hearts are full of many
evils. While their hatred may be concealed by
trickery, their wrongdoing will be exposed in
public.

PROVERBS 26:24–26 NLT

KEEPING SHORT ACCOUNTS

■ Then Peter came to Jesus and asked, "Lord, how many times shall I forgive my brother when he sins against me? Up to seven times?"

Jesus answered, "I tell you, not seven times, but seventy-seven times."

MATTHEW 18:21–22 NIV

■ But I tell you: Love your enemies and pray for those who persecute you.

MATTHEW 5:44 NIV

■ Whenever you stand up to pray, you must forgive what others have done to you . Then your Father in heaven will forgive your sins.

MARK 11:25 CEV

■ Be kind and compassionate to one another,
forgiving each other, just as in Christ God
forgave you.

EPHESIANS 4:32 NIV

■ Bear with each other and forgive whatever
grievances you may have against one another.
Forgive as the Lord forgave you.

COLOSSIANS 3:13 NIV

■ Dear friends, let us continue to love one
another, for love comes from God. Anyone
who loves is a child of God and knows God.
But anyone who does not love does not
know God, for God is love.

1 JOHN 4:7–8 NLT

■ The Lord passed in front of Moses, calling out, "Yahweh! The LORD! The God of compassion and mercy! I am slow to anger and filled with unfailing love and faithfulness."

EXODUS 34:6 NLT

■ "But love your enemies, do good to them, and lend to them without expecting to get anything back. Then your reward will be great, and you will be sons of the Most High, because he is kind to the ungrateful and wicked. Be merciful, just as your Father is merciful.

Do not judge, and you will not be judged. Do not condemn, and you will not be condemned. Forgive, and you will be forgiven. Give, and it will be given to you. A good measure, pressed down, shaken together and running over, will be poured into your lap. For with the measure you use, it will be measured to you."

LUKE 6:35–38 NIV

CONFRONTING ABUSE

■ "You're blessed when you feel you've lost
what is most dear to you. Only then can you
be embraced by the One most dear to you."

MATTHEW 5:4 MSG

■ A prudent person foresees danger and takes
precautions. The simpleton goes blindly on
and suffers the consequences.

PROVERBS 22:3 NLT

■ Yet what we suffer now is nothing compared
to the glory he will reveal to us later.

ROMANS 8:18 NLT

■ "I have told you these things, so that in me you may have peace. In this world you will have trouble. But take heart! I have overcome the world."

JOHN 16:33 NIV

■ I can do everything through him who gives me strength.

PHILIPPIANS 4:13 NIV

■ God gave us a spirit not of fear but of power and love and self-control.

2 TIMOTHY 1:7 ESV

■ On that day you will be glad, even if you have to go through many hard trials for a while. Your faith will be like gold that has been tested in a fire. And these trials will prove that your faith is worth much more than gold that can be destroyed. They will show that you will be given praise and honor and glory when Jesus Christ returns. You have never seen Jesus, and you don't see him now. But still you love him and have faith in him, and no words can tell how glad and happy you are to be saved. That's why you have faith.

1 PETER 1:6–9 CEV

■ Be brave and strong! Don't be afraid of the nations on the other side of the Jordan. The LORD your God will always be at your side, and he will never abandon you.

DEUTERONOMY 31:6 CEV

■ Don't be afraid. I am with you.
Don't tremble with fear.
I am your God.
I will make you strong,
     as I protect you with my arm
     and give you victories.

ISAIAH 41:10 CEV

■ Be fair to the poor and to orphans.
Defend the helpless and everyone in need.

PSALM 82:3 CEV

■ The LORD will lead you into the land. He will
always be with you and help you, so don't
ever be afraid of your enemies.

DEUTERONOMY 31:8 CEV

■ "Peace I leave with you; my peace I give you.
I do not give to you as the world gives.
Do not let your hearts be troubled and
do not be afraid."

JOHN 14:27 NIV

■ The angel of the Lord encamps around those
who fear him, and delivers them.

PSALM 34:7 NRSV

GETTING HELP

■ But God has so composed the body, giving greater honor to the part that lacked it, that there may be no division in the body, but that the members may have the same care for one another. If one member suffers, all suffer together; if one member is honored, all rejoice together.

1 CORINTHIANS 12:24–26 ESV

■ "Have I not commanded you? Be strong and courageous. Do not be terrified; do not be discouraged, for the LORD your God will be with you wherever you go."

JOSHUA 1:9 NIV

■ And if God cares so wonderfully for flowers
  that are here today and thrown into the fire
  tomorrow, he will certainly care for you.
  Why do you have so little faith?

LUKE 12:28 NLT

■ I look up to the mountains; does my strength
      come from mountains?
  No, my strength comes from God,
      who made heaven, and earth,
      and mountains.

PSALM 121:1–2 MSG

■ I, your God, have a firm grip on you and
      I'm not letting go.
  I'm telling you, "Don't panic.
  I'm right here to help you."

ISAIAH 41:13 MSG

■ The LORD is my rock, my fortress and
my deliverer; my God is my rock,
in whom I take refuge.
He is my shield and the horn of my
salvation, my stronghold.

PSALM 18:2 NIV

■ People of Jerusalem, you don't need to cry
anymore. The Lord is kind, and as soon as he
hears your cries for help, he will come.

ISAIAH 30:19 CEV

■ For he will command his angels concerning
you to guard you in all your ways.

PSALM 91:11 NIV

■ You are my hiding place; you will protect me from trouble and surround me with songs of deliverance.

PSALM 32:7 NIV

■ When you pass through the waters, I will be with you and when you pass through the rivers, they will not sweep over you.

When you walk through the fire, you will not be burned; the flames will not set you ablaze.

ISAIAH 43:2 NIV

■ Though you have made me see troubles, many and bitter, you will restore my life again; from the depths of the earth you will again bring me up.

PSALM 71:20 NIV

■ Therefore we do not lose heart. Though outwardly we are wasting away, yet inwardly we are being renewed day by day.

2 CORINTHIANS 4:16 NIV

■ God is our refuge and strength, an ever-present help in trouble.

Therefore we will not fear, though the earth give way and the mountains fall into the heart of the sea, though its waters roar and foam and the mountains quake with their surging.

PSALM 46:1–3 NIV

■ "For I know the plans I have for you," declares the LORD, "plans to prosper you and not to harm you, plans to give you hope and a future."

JEREMIAH 29:11 NIV

■ Pile your troubles on God's shoulders—
      he'll carry your load, he'll help you out.
He'll never let good people topple into ruin.

PSALM 55:22 MSG

■ Praise be to the Lord, to God our Savior,
      who daily bears our burdens.

PSALM 68:19 NIV

■ "The LORD is my rock and my fortress and
my deliverer."

2 SAMUEL 22:2 NKJV

■ You hear, O LORD, the desire of the afflicted;
you encourage them, and you listen to
their cry.

PSALM 10:17 NIV

RECOVERING FROM ABUSE

■ By his wounds you are healed.

1 PETER 2:24 NLT

■ The thief comes only to steal and kill and destroy; I have come that they may have life, and have it to the full.

JOHN 10:10 NIV

■ May our Lord Jesus Christ himself and God our Father, who loved us and by his grace gave us eternal encouragement and good hope, encourage your hearts and strengthen you in every good deed and word.

2 THESSALONIANS 2:16–17 NIV

■ He heals the brokenhearted and binds up
their wounds.

PSALM 147:3 NIV

■ Be strong and take heart,
    all you who hope in the LORD.

PSALM 31:24 NIV

■ The Spirit of God, who raised Jesus from
the dead, lives in you. And just as God raised
Christ Jesus from the dead, he will give life to
your mortal bodies by this same Spirit living
within you.

ROMANS 8:11 NLT

■ Yet what we suffer now is nothing compared
to the glory he will reveal to us later.

ROMANS 8:18 NLT

■ On that day you will be glad, even if you have to go through many hard trials for a while. Your faith will be like gold that has been tested in a fire. And these trials will prove that your faith is worth much more than gold that can be destroyed. They will show that you will be given praise and honor and glory when Jesus Christ returns. You have never seen Jesus, and you don't see him now. But still you love him and have faith in him, and no words can tell how glad and happy you are to be saved. That's why you have faith.

1 PETER 1:6–9 CEV

ONE MOMENT
AT A TIME

FINDING SAFETY

1. If you're in an abusive relationship, reject the lies your spouse feeds you. You did not bring the abuse on yourself. You don't deserve to take the brunt of anger. You do deserve to be treated with respect.

2. Forgiveness doesn't mean living with abuse. Forgiveness doesn't mean it's okay for someone else to treat you abusively. Love your spouse enough to confront the sin and refuse to live with it.

3. Don't isolate yourself. Reach out until you find someone who really listens, understands, and takes steps to help you.

4. If you feel afraid for your physical safety, get out fast. God has given you an internal warning system—listen to it. Take immediate measures to protect yourself and develop a safe plan for getting out. If you need help, call an agency such as The National Domestic Violence Hotline.

CHAPTER 7

SEX AND INTIMACY

I've learned that the words sex and intimacy are not interchangeable. While many people describe sex as "being intimate," it's really only intimacy if it reflects what comes out of your heart. Sex can be a picture of the intimate closeness, vulnerability, tenderness, and concern that exists between partners. I've also learned, though, that it's possible to become intimate with someone when there's no sex involved. Recently I found myself letting my heart become intimate with a co-worker. While we haven't done anything physically inappropriate, I realize I've crossed an emotional line I should have reserved for my wife.

■ Don, age 30, Illinois ■

LIVING INTIMATELY

■ Place me like a seal over your heart,
      like a seal on your arm;
for love is as strong as death,
      its jealousy unyielding as the grave.
It burns like blazing fire,
      like a mighty flame.

SONG OF SOLOMON 8:6 NIV

■ Fulfill my joy by being like-minded, having the same love, being of one accord, of one mind.

PHILIPPIANS 2:2 NKJV

■ If a man has recently married, he must not be sent to war or have any other duty laid on him. For one year he is to be free to stay at home and bring happiness to the wife he has married.

DEUTERONOMY 24:5 NIV

■ The LORD God said, "It is not good for the man to be alone. I will make a helper suitable for him."

So the LORD God caused the man to fall into a deep sleep; and while he was sleeping, he took one of the man's ribs and closed up the place with flesh. Then the LORD God made a woman from the rib he had taken out of the man, and he brought her to the man.

The man said,
"This is now bone of my bones and flesh of my flesh; she shall be called 'woman,' for she was taken out of man."

For this reason a man will leave his father and mother and be united to his wife, and they will become one flesh.

GENESIS 2:18, 21–24 NIV

ENJOYING SEX

■ My lover is mine, and I am his.
  Nightly he strolls in our garden,
      Delighting in the flowers

SONG OF SOLOMON 2:16 MSG

■ May your fountain be blessed,
      and may you rejoice in the wife of
      your youth.
  A loving doe, a graceful deer—
      may her breasts satisfy you always,
      may you ever be captivated by her love.

PROVERBS 5:18–19 NIV

■ Let him kiss me with the kisses of his mouth!
      For your love is better than wine.

SONG OF SOLOMON 1:2 ESV

■ But because there is so much sexual immorality, each man should have his own wife, and each woman should have her own husband. The husband should fulfill his wife's sexual needs, and the wife should fulfill her husband's needs. The wife gives authority over her body to her husband, and the husband gives authority over his body to his wife. Do not deprive each other of sexual relations, unless you both agree to refrain from sexual intimacy for a limited time so you can give yourselves more completely to prayer. Afterward, you should come together again so that Satan won't be able to tempt you because of your lack of self-control.

1 CORINTHIANS 7:2–5 NLT

■ I belong to my lover,
and his desire is for me.

SONG OF SOLOMON 7:10 NIV

■ As an apricot tree stands out in the forest,
    my lover stands above the young men
    in town.
All I want is to sit in his shade,
    to taste and savor his delicious love.

SONG OF SOLOMON 2:3 MSG

MAINTAINING PURITY

■ Honor marriage, and guard the sacredness of sexual intimacy between wife and husband. God draws a firm line against casual and illicit sex.

HEBREWS 13:4 MSG

■ The acts of the sinful nature are obvious: sexual immorality, impurity and debauchery.

GALATIANS 5:19 NIV

■ Put to death, therefore, whatever belongs to your earthly nature: sexual immorality, impurity, lust, evil desires and greed, which is idolatry.

COLOSSIANS 3:5 NIV

■ Instead, clothe yourself with the presence of the Lord Jesus Christ. And don't let yourself think about ways to indulge your evil desires.

ROMANS 13:14 NLT

■ Run from anything that stimulates youthful lusts. Instead, pursue righteous living, faithfulness, love, and peace. Enjoy the companionship of those who call on the Lord with pure hearts.

2 TIMOTHY 2:22 NLT

■ Flee from sexual immorality. Every other sin a person commits is outside the body, but the sexually immoral person sins against his own body.

1 CORINTHIANS 6:18 ESV

■ But immorality or any impurity or greed must not even be named among you, as is proper among saints.

EPHESIANS 5:3 NASB

■ So behave properly, as people do in the day. Don't go to wild parties or get drunk or be vulgar or indecent. Don't quarrel or be jealous.

ROMANS 13:13 CEV

■ Don't you realize that your body is the temple of the Holy Spirit, who lives in you and was given to you by God? You do not belong to yourself, for God bought you with a high price. So you must honor God with your body.

1 CORINTHIANS 6:19–20 NLT

■ But now you must be holy in everything you do, just as God who chose you is holy. For the Scriptures say, "You must be holy because I am holy."

1 PETER 1:15–16 NLT

■ God didn't choose you to be filthy, but to be pure.

1 THESSALONIANS 4:7 CEV

■ God's will is for you to be holy, so stay away from all sexual sin.

1 THESSALONIANS 4:3 NLT

■ But each person is tempted when he is lured and enticed by his own desire.

JAMES 1:14 ESV

■ But I tell you that anyone who looks at a woman lustfully has already committed adultery with her in his heart.

MATTHEW 5:28 NIV

WARNINGS AGAINST UNFAITHFULNESS

■ For these commands are a lamp, this teaching is a light, and the corrections of discipline are the way to life, keeping you from the immoral woman, from the smooth tongue of the wayward wife.

Do not lust in your heart after her beauty or let her captivate you with her eyes, for the prostitute reduces you to a loaf of bread, and the adulteress preys upon your very life.

Can a man scoop fire into his lap without his clothes being burned?

Can a man walk on hot coals without his feet being scorched?

So is he who sleeps with another man's wife; no one who touches her will go unpunished.

PROVERBS 6:23–29 NIV

■ My son, pay close attention and don't forget what I tell you to do. . . .

From the window of my house, I once happened to see some foolish young men. . . .

One of these young men turned the corner and was walking by the house of an unfaithful wife.

She was dressed fancy like a woman of the street with only one thing in mind. . . .

She grabbed him and kissed him, and with no sense of shame, she said:

". . .Let's go there [on my bed] and make love all night.

My husband is traveling, and he's far away. . . ."

And so, she tricked him with all of her sweet talk and her flattery.

Right away he followed her like an ox on the way to be slaughtered, or like a fool on the way to be punished and killed with arrows.

He was no more than a bird rushing into

a trap, without knowing it would cost him his life.

My son, pay close attention to what I have said.

Don't even think about that kind of woman or let yourself be misled by someone like her.

Such a woman has caused the downfall and destruction of a lot of men.

Her house is a one-way street leading straight down to the world of the dead.

PROVERBS 1, 6, 9–10, 13, 18–19, 21–27 CEV

■ The mouth of an immoral woman is a deep pit; He who is abhorred by the LORD will fall there.

PROVERBS 22:14 NKJV

■ Now then, my sons, listen to me;
>   do not turn aside from what I say.
Keep to a path far from her,
>   do not go near the door of her house...
Drink water from your own cistern,
>   running water from your own well.
Should your springs overflow in the streets,
>   your streams of water in the public
>   squares?
Let them be yours alone,
>   never to be shared with strangers.
May your fountain be blessed,
>   and may you rejoice in the wife of
>   your youth.
A loving doe, a graceful deer—
>   may her breasts satisfy you always,
>   may you ever be captivated by her love.
Why be captivated, my son, by an adulteress?
>   Why embrace the bosom of another
>   man's wife?
For a man's ways are in full view of the LORD,
>   and he examines all his paths.

135

The evil deeds of a wicked man ensnare him;
    the cords of his sin hold him fast.
He will die for lack of discipline,
    led astray by his own great folly.

Proverbs 5:7–8, 15–23 NIV

GUARDING AGAINST IMMORALITY

■ Be self-controlled and alert. Your enemy the devil prowls around like a roaring lion looking for someone to devour. Resist him, standing firm in the faith, because you know that your brothers throughout the world are undergoing the same kind of sufferings.

And the God of all grace, who called you to his eternal glory in Christ, after you have suffered a little while, will himself restore you and make you strong, firm and steadfast.

1 PETER 5:8–10 NIV

■ So humble yourselves before God. Resist the devil, and he will flee from you.

JAMES 4:7 NLT

■ No testing has overtaken you that is not common to everyone. God is faithful, and he will not let you be tested beyond your strength, but with the testing he will also provide the way out so that you may be able to endure it.

1 CORINTHIANS 10:13 NRSV

■ Blessed is anyone who endures temptation. Such a one has stood the test and will receive the crown of life that the Lord has promised to those who love him. No one, when tempted, should say, "I am being tempted by God"; for God cannot be tempted by evil and he himself tempts no one.

JAMES 1:12–13 NRSV

■ My brothers and sisters, whenever you face trials of any kind, consider it nothing but joy, because you know that the testing of your faith produces endurance.

JAMES 1:2–3 NRSV

■ For we do not have a high priest who is unable to sympathize with our weaknesses, but we have one who has been tempted in every way, just as we are—yet was without sin. Let us then approach the throne of grace with confidence, so that we may receive mercy and find grace to help us in our time of need.

HEBREWS 4:15–16 NIV

■ How can a young man keep his way pure?
    By living according to your word.
I seek you with all my heart; do not let me
    stray from your commands.
I have hidden your word in my heart
    that I might not sin against you.

PSALM 119:9–11 NIV

■ Finally, brothers, whatever is true, whatever
is noble, whatever is right, whatever is pure,
whatever is lovely, whatever is admirable—if
anything is excellent or praiseworthy—think
about such things.

PHILIPPIANS 4:8 NIV

■ With all your heart you must trust the LORD
and not your own judgment.
    Always let him lead you, and he will clear
the road for you to follow.

PROVERBS 3:5–6 CEV

■ Let us not become weary in doing good, for at the proper time we will reap a harvest if we do not give up. Therefore, as we have opportunity, let us do good to all people, especially to those who belong to the family of believers.

GALATIANS 6:9–10 NIV

■ Those who live according to the sinful nature have their minds set on what that nature desires; but those who live in accordance with the Spirit have their minds set on what the Spirit desires.

ROMANS 8:5 NIV

■ Put on all the armor that God gives, so you can defend yourself against the devil's tricks.

EPHESIANS 6:11 CEV

■ As obedient children, do not conform to
the evil desires you had when you lived in
ignorance.

1 PETER 1:14 NIV

■ Train me in good common sense; I'm
thoroughly committed to living your way.

PSALM 119:66 MSG

■ For the grace of God that brings salvation has
appeared to all men. It teaches us to say "No"
to ungodliness and worldly passions, and to
live self-controlled, upright and godly lives in
this present age.

TITUS 2:11–12 NIV

■ For sin shall not be master over you, for you
are not under law but under grace.

ROMANS 6:14 NASB

■ For this reason, since the day we heard about you, we have not stopped praying for you and asking God to fill you with the knowledge of his will through all spiritual wisdom and understanding. And we pray this in order that you may live a life worthy of the Lord and may please him in every way: bearing fruit in every good work, growing in the knowledge of God, being strengthened with all power according to his glorious might so that you may have great endurance and patience, and joyfully giving thanks to the Father, who has qualified you to share in the inheritance of the saints in the kingdom of light.

COLOSSIANS 1:9–12 NIV

■ And now that Jesus has suffered and was tempted, he can help anyone else who is tempted.

HEBREWS 2:18 CEV

ONE MOMENT
AT A TIME

KEEPING YOUR
MARRIAGE
PURE

1. Broaden your definition of intimacy. Being intimate with someone is much more than just the physical relationship. Save your body—and your heart—for the one to whom it belongs. Just as bodies become intertwined, work on letting your hearts and lives reflect that same closeness.

2. Talk about it. The subject of sex can be sensitive for many couples. Find a way to talk about it even if it is awkward at first. Define expectations, explain interests, and share your

frustrations. If you're too embarrassed to talk about it, you will not solve the problems you need to discuss.

3. Fight for purity. Sin is often enjoyable at the moment, and lust is no exception. Giving in to it, however, leads to guilt, strained intimacy, and resentfulness when your spouse doesn't live up to unreasonable fantasies you've enjoyed. Steer clear of places, books, internet sites, or people who lure you into this temptation.

CHAPTER 8

YOU AND YOUR FAMILY

My marriage has another woman in it. In fact, my wife encourages it. We frequently have her over and we leave our kids with her. Sound strange? The other woman is my mother-in-law. You'd think that with how quickly that we go along with her opinions, that she is an equal partner in our marriage. I've tried to talk to my wife about it and she says she agrees with me, but she's just not willing to stand up to her mom or set appropriate boundaries.

■ Carl, age 38, Connecticut ■

SHARING GOD'S PERSPECTIVE ON CHILDREN

■ Children are a gift from the LORD; they are
a reward from him.
Children born to a young man are like
arrows in a warrior's hands.
How joyful is the man whose quiver is
full of them! He will not be put to
shame when he confronts his accusers
at the city gates.

PSALM 127:3–5 NLT

■ For you created my inmost being;
> you knit me together in my mother's
> womb.

I praise you because I am fearfully
> and wonderfully made;
> your works are wonderful,
> I know that full well.

My frame was not hidden from you
> when I was made in the secret place.

When I was woven together in the depths
> of the earth, your eyes saw my
> unformed body.

All the days ordained for me were written
> in your book before one of them
> came to be.

PSALM 139:13–16 NIV

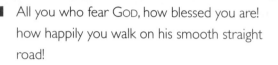

■ All you who fear GOD, how blessed you are! how happily you walk on his smooth straight road!

You worked hard and deserve all you've got coming.

Enjoy the blessing! Revel in the goodness!

Your wife will bear children as a vine bears grapes, your household lush as a vineyard.

The children around your table as fresh and promising as young olive shoots.

Stand in awe of God's Yes.

Oh, how he blesses the one who fears GOD!

PSALM 128:1–4 MSG

BEING INTENTIONAL ABOUT PARENTING

■ Train up a child in the way he should go;
even when he is old he will not depart
from it.

PROVERBS 22:6 ESV

■ "But watch out! Be careful never to forget
what you yourself have seen. Do not let
these memories escape from your mind as
long as you live! And be sure to pass them
on to your children and grandchildren. Never
forget the day when you stood before the
LORD your God at Mount Sinai, where he told
me, 'Summon the people before me, and I
will personally instruct them. Then they will
learn to fear me as long as they live, and they
will teach their children to fear me also.' "

DEUTERONOMY 4:9–10 NLT

WHAT THE BIBLE SAYS ABOUT MARRIAGE

■ Memorize his laws and tell them to your
children over and over again. Talk about
them all the time, whether you're at home
or walking along the road or going to bed
at night, or getting up in the morning. Write
down copies and tie them to your wrists
and foreheads to help you obey them. Write
these laws on the door frames of your
homes and on your town gates.

DEUTERONOMY 6:6–9 CEV

■ "For I have chosen him, so that he will
direct his children and his household after
him to keep the way of the LORD by doing
what is right and just, so that the LORD will
bring about for Abraham what he has
promised him."

GENESIS 18:19 NIV

■ "But if serving the LORD seems undesirable to you, then choose for yourselves this day whom you will serve, whether the gods your forefathers served beyond the River, or the gods of the Amorites, in whose land you are living. But as for me and my household, we will serve the LORD."

JOSHUA 24:15 NIV

■ And how from infancy you have known the holy Scriptures, which are able to make you wise for salvation through faith in Christ Jesus.

2 TIMOTHY 3:15 NIV

■ Fathers, do not provoke your children to anger, but bring them up in the discipline and instruction of the Lord.

EPHESIANS 6:4 ESV

SERVING TOGETHER

■ "You must present as the LORD's portion the best and holiest part of everything given to you."

NUMBERS 18:29 NIV

■ Jesus sat down near the collection box in the Temple and watched as the crowds dropped in their money. Many rich people put in large amounts. Then a poor widow came and dropped in two small coins. Jesus called his disciples to him and said, "I tell you the truth, this poor widow has given more than all the others who are making contributions. For they gave a tiny part of their surplus, but she, poor as she is, has given everything she had to live on."

MARK 12:41–44 NLT

■ Those who are generous are blessed,
   for they share their bread with the poor.

PROVERBS 22:9 NRSV

■ For truly, I say to you, whoever gives you a
cup of water to drink because you belong to
Christ will by no means lose his reward.

MARK 9:41 ESV

■ Give freely and spontaneously. Don't have
a stingy heart. The way you handle matters
like this triggers GOD, your God's, blessing in
everything you do, all your work and ven-
tures. There are always going to be poor and
needy people among you. So I command you:
Always be generous, open purse and hands,
give to your neighbors in trouble, your poor
and hurting neighbors.

DEUTERONOMY 15:10–11 MSG

■ When God's people are in need, be ready to help them. Always be eager to practice hospitality.

ROMANS 12:13 NLT

ENFORCING DISCIPLINE

■ Young people are prone to foolishness and fads; the cure comes through tough-minded discipline.

PROVERBS 22:15 MSG

■ Correct your children before it's too late; if you don't punish them, you are destroying them.

PROVERBS 19:18 CEV

■ He who spares the rod hates his son, but he who loves him is careful to discipline him.

PROVERBS 13:24 NIV

■ And you have forgotten that word of encouragement that addresses you as sons:

"My son, do not make light of the Lord's discipline, and do not lose heart when he rebukes you, because the Lord disciplines those he loves, and he punishes everyone he accepts as a son."

Endure hardship as discipline; God is treating you as sons. For what son is not disciplined by his father? If you are not disciplined (and everyone undergoes discipline), then you are illegitimate children and not true sons. Moreover, we have all had human fathers who disciplined us and we respected them for it. How much more should we submit to the Father of our spirits and live! Our fathers disciplined us for a little while as they thought best; but God disciplines us for our good, that we may share in his holiness. No discipline seems pleasant at the time, but painful. Later on,

however, it produces a harvest of righteousness and peace for those who have been
trained by it.

HEBREWS 12:5–11 NIV

■ Don't be afraid to correct your young ones;
    a spanking won't kill them.
A good spanking, in fact, might save them
    from something worse than death.

PROVERBS 23:13–14 MSG

■ To discipline a child produces wisdom,
but a mother is disgraced by an undisciplined
child.

PROVERBS 29:15 NLT

HONORING PARENTS

■ "Honor your father and your mother,
so that you may live long in the land the
LORD your God is giving you."

EXODUS 20:12 NIV

■ But if a widow has children or grandchildren,
these should learn first of all to put their
religion into practice by caring for their own
family and so repaying their parents and
grandparents, for this is pleasing to God.

1 TIMOTHY 5:4 NIV

■ Grandchildren are the crown of the aged,
and the glory of children is their parents.

PROVERBS 17:6 NRSV

■ A wise son makes a glad father,
But a foolish son is the grief of his mother.

PROVERBS 10:1 NKJV

■ But standing by the cross of Jesus were his
mother and his mother's sister, Mary the wife
of Clopas, and Mary Magdalene. When Jesus
saw his mother and the disciple whom he
loved standing nearby, he said to his mother,
"Woman, behold, your son!" Then he said to
the disciple, "Behold, your mother!" And from
that hour the disciple took her to his own
home.

JOHN 19:25–27 ESV

■ If anyone does not provide for his relatives,
and especially for his immediate family,
he has denied the faith and is worse than
an unbeliever.

1 TIMOTHY 5:8 NIV

■ Anyone who steals from his father and mother and says, "What's wrong with that?" is no better than a murderer.

PROVERBS 28:24 NLT

■ If any believing woman has relatives who are widows, let her care for them. Let the church not be burdened, so that it may care for those who are truly widows.

1 TIMOTHY 5:16 ESV

■ The women said to Naomi: "Praise be to the LORD, who this day has not left you. . . . For your daughter-in-law, who loves you and who is better to you than seven sons."

RUTH 4:14 – 15 NIV

■ My child, listen when your father corrects you. Don't neglect your mother's instruction.

PROVERBS 1:8 NLT

■ For God commanded, "Honor your father and your mother," and, "Whoever reviles father or mother must surely die." But you say, " If anyone tells his father or his mother, 'What you would have gained from me is given to God,' he need not honor his father." So for the sake of your tradition you have made void the word of God.

MATTHEW 15:4–6 ESV

■ Listen to your father, who gave you life, and do not despise your mother when she is old.

PROVERBS 23:22 NIV

ONE MOMENT AT A TIME

LOVING YOUR CHILDREN

■ 1. Don't leave it to chance. Identify character traits you would like to see developed in your children. Create a specific plan to help make those changes a reality.

■ 2. Build a relationship. If you own a dog, you can probably get the animal to toe the line with a combination of positive and negative reinforcements. Kids, however, need much, much more. Work hard at being more than the general who snaps orders and expects full compliance. Get to know your kids, listen to them, and create an atmosphere that is both tailored to their success and that encourages obedience.

3. Build a support system. One hundred years ago, a typical family might have had a few generations (and perhaps some extended family) living nearby or even under the same roof. In those days, finding support, getting advice, and soliciting help was easy. Today's families are very different. Make sure you have a network you can compare notes and exchange ideas with. Find a group that you can be honest with—without feeling the need to compete with them.

4. Honor your own parents. The Bible's command to honor our parents does not come with an age limit. No matter how you feel about them, the office of parent should be respected.

CHAPTER 9

TRAITS OF A STRONG MARRIAGE

It took a while, but I finally found the secret to a good marriage. It's actually pretty simple: I had to realize that it's not about me. When I go through our routine by looking out for her (her needs, her choices, her preferences), I find we really start to click. Yes, I end up living a life of sacrifice, but I'd say we finally have a great marriage. And if you think I'm nothing but a doormat, then you haven't seen the whole picture. What I've found is that the more I give, the more she gives in return. Honestly, life has never been better.

■ Robert, age 57, Texas ■

CHOOSING A JOYFUL SPIRIT

■ Be joyful in hope, patient in affliction,
    faithful in prayer.

ROMANS 12:12 NIV

■ Be glad in the LORD and rejoice,
    you righteous ones;
And shout for joy, all you who are upright
    in heart.

PSALM 32:11 NASB

■ In him our hearts rejoice, for we trust in his
holy name.

PSALM 33:21 NLT

■ For the kingdom of God is not a matter of eating and drinking, but of righteousness, peace and joy in the Holy Spirit.

ROMANS 14:17 NIV

■ Then my soul will rejoice in the LORD,
    exulting in his salvation.

PSALM 35:9 ESV

■ Make a joyful noise to the LORD, all the earth!

PSALM 100:1 ESV

■ Rejoice in the Lord always. I will say it again: Rejoice!

PHILIPPIANS 4:4 NIV

■ Rejoice always.

1 THESSALONIANS 5:16 ESV

■ The precepts of the LORD are right, rejoicing
the heart;
The commandment of the LORD is pure,
enlightening the eyes.

PSALM 19:8 NASB

■ But I trust in your unfailing love;
my heart rejoices in your salvation.

PSALM 13:5 NIV

■ May the God of hope fill you with all joy
and peace as you trust in him, so that you
may overflow with hope by the power of
the Holy Spirit.

ROMANS 15:13 NIV

■ I will be glad and exult in you;
   I will sing praise to your name,
   O Most High.

PSALM 9:2 NRSV

■ You have put gladness in my heart.

PSALM 4:7 NKJV

■ Worship God in adoring embrace,
   Celebrate in trembling awe.

PSALM 2:11 MSG

■ These things I have spoken to you,
   that my joy may be in you,
   and that your joy may be full.

JOHN 15:11 ESV

FEELING SECURE IN YOUR IDENTITY IN CHRIST

■ For you are all children of God through faith in Christ Jesus.

GALATIANS 3:26 NLT

■ All this is from God, who reconciled us to himself through Christ and gave us the ministry of reconciliation: that God was reconciling the world to himself in Christ, not counting men's sins against them. And he has committed to us the message of reconciliation. We are therefore Christ's ambassadors, as though God were making his appeal through us. We implore you on Christ's behalf: Be reconciled to God. God made him who had no sin to be sin for us, so that in him we might become the righteousness of God.

2 CORINTHIANS 5:18–21 NIV

■ But to all who did receive him, who believed in his name, he gave the right to become children of God.

JOHN 1:12 ESV

■ For all who are led by the Spirit of God are children of God. So you have not received a spirit that makes you fearful slaves. Instead, you received God's Spirit when he adopted you as his own children. Now we call him, "Abba, Father."

ROMANS 8:14–15 NLT

■ I no longer call you servants, because a servant does not know his master's business. Instead, I have called you friends, for everything that I learned from my Father I have made known to you.

JOHN 15:15 NIV

■ Praise the God and Father of our Lord Jesus Christ for the spiritual blessings that Christ has brought us from heaven! Before the world was created, God had Christ choose us to live with him and to be his holy and innocent and loving people. God was kind and decided that Christ would choose us to be God's own adopted children. God was very kind to us because of the Son he dearly loves, and so we should praise God.

EPHESIANS 1:3–6 CEV

KNOWING YOUR SELF-WORTH

■ How precious are your thoughts about me,
O God. They cannot be numbered! I can't
even count them; they outnumber the grains
of sand! And when I wake up, you are still
with me!

PSALM 139:17–18 NLT

■ "Before I shaped you in the womb,
    I knew all about you.
Before you saw the light of day,
    I had holy plans for you:
A prophet to the nations—
    that's what I had in mind for you."

JEREMIAH 1:5 MSG

■ He gave his life to free us from every kind of sin, to cleanse us, and to make us his very own people, totally committed to doing good deeds.

TITUS 2:14 NLT

■ "For the LORD your God is living among you. He is a mighty savior. He will take delight in you with gladness. With his love, he will calm all your fears. He will rejoice over you with joyful songs."

ZEPHANIAH 3:17 NLT

REMAINING HUMBLE

■ So, if you think you are standing firm,
  be careful that you don't fall!

  1 Corinthians 10:12 niv

■ Humble yourselves, therefore, under the
  mighty hand of God so that at the proper
  time he may exalt you.

  1 Peter 5:6 esv

■ The Lord sustains the humble
  but casts the wicked to the ground.

  Psalm 147:6 niv

■ For the Lord delights in his people;
  he crowns the humble with victory.

  Psalm 149:4 nlt

■ For my part, I am going to boast about nothing but the Cross of our Master, Jesus Christ. Because of that Cross, I have been crucified in relation to the world, set free from the stifling atmosphere of pleasing others and fitting into the little patterns that they dictate.

GALATIANS 6:14 MSG

■ Let another praise you, and not your own mouth; someone else, and not your own lips.

PROVERBS 27:2 NIV

■ "Blessed are the poor in spirit,
    For theirs is the kingdom of heaven."

MATTHEW 5:3 NKJV

■ He has showed you, O man, what is good.
    And what does the LORD require of you?
To act justly and to love mercy
    and to walk humbly with your God.

MICAH 6:8 NIV

■ Because of the privilege and authority God
has given me, I give each of you this warning:
Don't think you are better than you really
are. Be honest in your evaluation of yourselves, measuring yourselves by the faith
God has given us.

ROMANS 12:3 NLT

DEALING WITH DIFFICULTIES

■ My flesh and my heart fail;
But God is the strength of my heart
and my portion forever.

PSALM 73:26 NKJV

■ Give all your worries and cares to God,
for he cares about you.

1 PETER 5:7 NLT

■ "The LORD will fight for you;
you need only to be still."

EXODUS 14:14 NIV

■ Trust in him at all times, O people;
pour out your hearts to him,
for God is our refuge.

PSALM 62:8 NIV

■ To him who is able to keep you from falling and to present you before his glorious presence without fault and with great joy— to the only God our Savior be glory, majesty, power and authority, through Jesus Christ our Lord, before all ages, now and forevermore!

JUDE 1:24–25 NIV

■ We are afflicted in every way, but not crushed; perplexed, but not driven to despair; persecuted, but not forsaken; struck down, but not destroyed; always carrying in the body the death of Jesus, so that the life of Jesus may also be manifested in our bodies.

2 CORINTHIANS 4:8–10 ESV

■ The LORD is close to the brokenhearted; he rescues those whose spirits are crushed.

PSALM 34:18 NLT

■ "Don't be afraid, I've redeemed you.

I've called your name. You're mine.

When you're in over your head,
I'll be there with you.

When you're in rough waters, you will
not go down.

When you're between a rock and a hard
place, it won't be a dead end—

Because I am God, your personal God,

The Holy of Israel, your Savior.

I paid a huge price for you: all of Egypt,
with rich Cush and Seba thrown in!

That's how much you mean to me!

That's how much I love you!

I'd sell off the whole world to get you
back, trade the creation just for you.

ISAIAH 43:1–2 MSG

FINDING STRENGTH IN CHRIST

■ Do you not know?
Have you not heard?
The LORD is the everlasting God,
    the Creator of the ends of the earth.
He will not grow tired or weary,
    and his understanding no one can
    fathom.
He gives strength to the weary
    and increases the power of the weak.
Even youths grow tired and weary,
    and young men stumble and fall;
but those who hope in the LORD
    will renew their strength.
They will soar on wings like eagles;
    they will run and not grow weary,
    they will walk and not be faint.

ISAIAH 40:28–31 NIV

■ Then Jesus said, "Come to me, all of you who are weary and carry heavy burdens, and I will give you rest. Take my yoke upon you. Let me teach you, because I am humble and gentle at heart, and you will find rest for your souls. For my yoke is easy to bear, and the burden I give you is light."

MATTHEW 11:28–30 NLT

■ But he replied, "My kindness is all you need. My power is strongest when you are weak." So if Christ keeps giving me his power, I will gladly brag about how weak I am. Yes, I am glad to be weak or insulted or mistreated or to have troubles and sufferings, if it is for Christ. Because when I am weak, I am strong.

2 CORINTHIANS 12:9–10 CEV

■ The LORD is my light and my salvation—
  whom shall I fear?
  The LORD is the stronghold of my life—
  of whom shall I be afraid? . . .
  Though an army besiege me, my heart will
  not fear; though war break out against
  me, even then will I be confident.

PSALM 27:1, 3 NIV

■ The eternal God is your refuge,
  and underneath are the everlasting arms.
  He will drive out your enemy before you.

DEUTERONOMY 33:27 NIV

■ When I felt my feet slipping, you came with
  your love and kept me steady.
  And when I was burdened with worries,
  you comforted me and made me feel
  secure.

PSALM 94:18–19 CEV

BEING GRATEFUL FOR WHAT GOD GIVES YOU

■ Shout with joy to the LORD, all the earth! Worship the LORD with gladness. Come before him, singing with joy. Acknowledge that the LORD is God! He made us, and we are his. We are his people, the sheep of his pasture. Enter his gates with thanksgiving; go into his courts with praise. Give thanks to him and praise his name.

PSALM 100:1–4 NLT

■ Offer to God a sacrifice of thanksgiving
And pay your vows to the Most High.

PSALM 50:14 NASB

■ Give thanks to the LORD, for he is good! His faithful love endures forever.

PSALM 107:1 NLT

GLORIFYING GOD TOGETHER

■ Give to the LORD, O families of the peoples,
   Give to the LORD glory and strength.

1 CHRONICLES 16:28 NKJV

■ Oh, magnify the LORD with me,
   and let us exalt his name together!

PSALM 34:3 ESV

■ Not to us, O Lord, not to us,
   but to your name give glory,
   for the sake of your steadfast love
   and your faithfulness!

PSALM 115:1 NRSV

■ So whether you eat or drink or whatever you do, do it all for the glory of God.

1 CORINTHIANS 10:31 NIV

■ You who fear the LORD, praise him!
All you offspring of Jacob, glorify him,
and stand in awe of him, all you offspring of Israel!

PSALM 22:23 ESV

■ Let me shout God's name with a praising song,
Let me tell his greatness in a prayer of thanks.

PSALM 69:30 MSG

■ I will praise you, O Lord my God, with all
    my heart;
I will glorify your name forever.

PSALM 86:12 NIV

■ You are my God, and I will give you thanks;
you are my God, and I will exalt you.

PSALM 118:28 NIV

ONE MOMENT
AT A TIME
CHOOSING
UNITY

■ 1. Be a giver. Giving is hard work, and putting someone else's needs ahead of your own is a difficult, conscious choice. Start small. Set reasonable goals on initial changes you can make.

■ 2. Don't be petty. It's easy to hold a grudge, bicker, and squabble over little things. Choose kindness instead and let offenses roll over you without hanging on to them.

■ 3. Do life together. Many married couples live under the same roof and communicate through complaining about life or bickering with each other. Take a different approach. Tackle life together. Work to stay on the same team and go face challenges together.

Look for all the
What the Bible Says About…
books from Barbour Publishing

What the Bible Says about
DIVORCE
ISBN 978-1-59789-995-6

What the Bible Says about
GRIEVING
ISBN 978-1-59789-994-9

What the Bible Says about
MONEY
ISBN 978-1-59789-992-5

192 pages / 3 ¾" × 6" / $4.97 each

Available wherever Christian books are sold.